Poetry for Kids

Carl Sandburg

POETRY FOR KIDS

Carl Sandburg

ILLUSTRATED BY
ROBERT CRAWFORD

EDITED BY KATHRYN BENZEL, PhD

MoonDance

Quarto is the authority on a wide range of topics.
Quarto educates, entertains, and enriches the lives of our readers—
enthusiasts and lovers of hands-on living.
www.quartoknows.com

This book is dedicated to my first granddaughter, Cecilia Rose Mettey. She came into our lives at just the right time! —R. C.
For my lovely grandchildren, readers all of them: Lucia, Josiah, Caleb, Noah —K. B.

MoonDance

6 Orchard Road, Suite 100
Lake Forest, CA 92630
quartoknows.com
Visit our blogs at quartoknows.com

Printed in China
1 3 5 7 9 10 8 6 4 2

MIX
Paper from
responsible sources
FSC® C101537

Contents

Introduction

It was a rainy gray afternoon in downtown Chicago, 1914. Carl Sandburg was huddled in a doorway waiting for the streetcar. He saw workers coming up from underground, in worn-out overalls, carrying their muddy shovels and lunch pails; the street vendors closing up their vegetable stands, counting their few pennies; garment workers walking slowly, their shoulders stooped, and heads hanging from twelve-hour work days; rich folk wearing their top hats in horse-drawn buggies, and new Ford automobiles buzzing around them. People's hats were blowing every which way in the slanted rain. Standing in the dreary weather, he remembered the warmth of his family and the prairie sunsets brilliant with red, orange, and yellow; harvesting farmers in the dust and sweat; and he reminisced about the whistling wind as he hung onto a boxcar as a hobo crossing the prairie. This is Carl Sandburg's poetry, filled with common Americans, the salt of the earth, working hard, living sparsely, laughing and singing a lot. He was the "Poet of the People," a spokesperson for "the mob, the crowd, the mass." He was the voice of early-20th-century American life.

Carl Sandburg was born on a cornstalk mattress in 1878 in Galesburg, Illinois, the land of Abraham Lincoln. It was America's Heartland, near Chicago's railroad intersection for American life. His parents were Swedish immigrants who never learned to read or write in English, struggling to support their seven children. Sandburg stopped his education after eighth grade to help with the family's income. He shined shoes, delivered milk and newspapers, and swept out bars and barbershops. In Chicago, he was introduced to the life and living that inspired his *Chicago Poems* (1916). At age nineteen in 1897, he hopped onto a boxcar heading west. On this trip, he discovered the breadth and beauty of the American landscape that would inspire his collections, *Cornhuskers* (1918) and *Smoke and Steel* (1920).

During his lifetime, Sandburg experienced the aftermath of the Civil War and saw the ravages of the 1960s Vietnam War. He saw the new Ford Model T in 1908 and the Ford Edsel in 1958. He lived through two depressions, including the Great Depression and the Dust Bowl. He endured two world wars. He witnessed the advent of television and was invited to fly on the first transcontinental flight from the East Coast to the West. He was a newspaper reporter, a lecturer, a biographer, and a folk singer. He won three Pulitzer Prizes for history and poetry.

Sandburg's experiences and observations are at the essence of his poetic vision, of the voice of the people. The underlying hope at the core of his poetry brings "tears for the tragic, love for the beautiful, laughter at folly, and silent, reverent contemplation of the common and everyday mysteries." He said, "Poetry is a mystic, sensuous mathematics of fire, smoke-stack, waffles, pansies, people, and purple sunsets. The capture of a picture, a song, a flair, in a deliberate prism of words."

He died in 1967 at 89, listening to Chopin and smelling the magnolias. His last word was "Paula," his wife's name.

Poems about People

Young Bullfrogs

Jimmy Wimbledon listened a first week in June.
Ditches along prairie roads of Northern Illinois
Filled the arch of night with young bullfrog songs.
Infinite mathematical metronomic croaks rose and spoke,
Rose and sang, rose in a choir of puzzles.
They made his head ache with riddles of music.
They rested his head with beaten cadence.
Jimmy Wimbledon listened.

Infinite — can't be measured because it never ends
metronomic — sounds like a device used to mark
musical time
cadence — rhythm in musical song or spoken speech

Weeds

From the time of the early radishes
To the time of the standing corn
Sleepy Henry Hackerman hoes.

There are laws in the village against weeds.
The law says a weed is wrong and shall be killed.
The weeds say life is a white and lovely thing
And the weeds come on and on in irrepressible regiments.
Sleepy Henry Hackerman hoes; and the village law uttering a ban
    on weeds is unchangeable law.

irrepressible — wild, disorderly
regiments — strong troops

Soup

I saw a famous man eating soup.
I say he was lifting a fat broth

Into his mouth with a spoon.
His name was in the newspapers that day

Spelled out in tall black headlines
And thousands of people were talking about him.

When I saw him,
He sat bending his head over a plate
Putting soup in his mouth with a spoon.

I Am the People, the Mob

I am the people — the mob — the crowd — the mass.

Do you know that all the great work of the world is done through me?

I am the workingman, the inventor, the maker of the world's food and clothes.

I am the audience that witnesses history. The Napoleons come from me and the Lincolns. They die. And then I send forth more Napoleons and Lincolns.

I am the seed ground. I am a prairie that will stand for much plowing. Terrible storms pass over me. I forget. The best of me is sucked out and wasted. I forget. Everything but Death comes to me and makes me work and give up what I have. And I forget.

Sometimes I growl, shake myself and spatter a few red drops for history to remember. Then — I forget.

When I, the People, learn to remember, when I, the People, use the lessons of yesterday and no longer forget who robbed me last year, who played me for a fool — then there will be no speaker in all the world say the name: "The People," with any fleck of a sneer in his voice or any far-off smile of derision.

The mob — the crowd — the mass — will arrive then.

Napoleons — Napoleon Bonaparte (1769-1821), French political leader,
emperor of France from 1804-1814
seed ground — cultivated land where crops are planted
sneer — expression of contempt

11

Shenandoah

In the Shenandoah Valley, one rider gray and one rider blue, and the sun
on the riders wondering.

Piled in the Shenandoah, riders blue and riders gray, piled with shovels,
one and another, dust in the Shenandoah taking them quicker than
mothers take children done with play.

The blue nobody remembers, the gray nobody remembers, it's all old and
old nowadays in the Shenandoah.

. . .

And all is young, a butter of dandelions slung on the turf, climbing blue
flowers of the wishing woodlands wondering: a midnight purple violet
claims the sun among old heads, among old dreams of repeating heads of a
rider blue and a rider gray in the Shenandoah.

Shenandoah Valley — West Virginia, site of Civil War battles (1861-1865)
rider gray — Confederate or Southern soldiers during Civil War
rider blue— Union or Northern soldiers during Civil War
slung — thrown about

Paula

Nothing else in this song — only your face.
Nothing else here — only your drinking, night-gray eyes.

The pier runs into the lake straight as a rifle barrel.
I stand on the pier and sing how I know you mornings.
It is not your eyes, your face, I remember.
It is not your dancing, race-horse feet.
It is something else I remember you for on the pier mornings.

Your hands are sweeter than nut-brown bread when you touch me.
Your shoulder brushes my arm — a south-west wind crosses the pier.
I forget your hands and your shoulder and I say again:

Nothing else in this song — only your face.
Nothing else here — only your drinking, night-gray eyes.

Paula — Carl's wife; they married in 1908.

Manual System

Mary has a thingamajig clamped on her ears
And sits all day taking plugs out and sticking plugs in.
Flashes and flashes — voices and voices
                         calling for ears to put words in
Faces at the ends of wires asking for other faces
                         at the ends of other wires:
All day taking plugs out and sticking plugs in,
Mary has a thingamajig clamped on her ears.

Manual System — Early telephone communication (1876-1904) used switchboard operators to connect callers. The caller would be connected to a central location, and the operator would plug that call into the person being called.
thingamajig — something hard to name

Jazz Fantasia

Drum on your drums, batter on your banjoes,
sob on the long cool winding saxophones.
Go to it, O jazzmen.

Sling your knuckles on the bottoms of the happy
tin pans, let your trombones ooze, and go husha-
husha-hush with the slippery sand-paper.

Moan like an autumn wind high in the lonesome treetops,
moan soft like you wanted somebody terrible, cry like a
racing car slipping away from a motorcycle cop, bang-bang!
you jazzmen, bang altogether drums, traps, banjoes, horns,
tin cans — make two people fight on the top of a stairway
and scratch each other's eyes in a clinch tumbling down the stairs.

Can the rough stuff . . . now a Mississippi steamboat pushes
up the night river with a hoo-hoo-hoo-oo . . . and the green
lanterns calling to the high soft stars . . . a red moon rides
on the humps of the low river hills . . . go to it, O jazzmen.

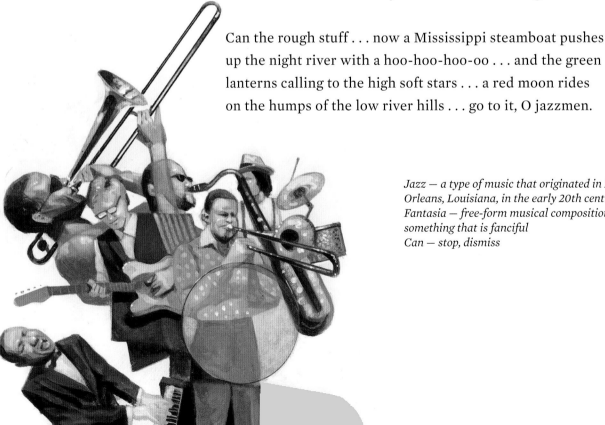

*Jazz — a type of music that originated in New
Orleans, Louisiana, in the early 20th century
Fantasia — free-form musical composition;
something that is fanciful
Can — stop, dismiss*

Illinois Farmer

Bury this old Illinois farmer with respect.
He slept the Illinois nights of his life after days of work in Illinois corn-
    fields.
Now he goes on a long sleep.
The wind he listened to in the cornsilk and tassels, the wind that
    combed his red beard zero mornings when snow lay white on the
    yellow ears in the bushel basket at the corncrib,
The same wind will now blow over the place here where his hands must
    dream of Illinois corn.

cornsilk — fine tassels on the top of ears of corn

Buffalo Bill

Boy heart of Johnny Jones — aching today?
Aching, and Buffalo Bill in town?
Buffalo Bill and ponies, cowboys, Indians?

Some of us know
All about it, Johnny Jones.

Buffalo Bill is a slanting look of the eyes,
    A slanting look under a hat on a horse.
He sits on a horse and a passing look is fixed
    On Johnny Jones, you and me, barelegged,
A slanting, passing, careless look under a hat on a horse.

Go clickety-clack, O pony hoofs along the street.
Come on and slant your eyes again, O Buffalo Bill.
Give us again the ache of our boy hearts.
Fill us again with the red love of prairies, dark nights, lonely wagons, and
    the crack-crack of rifles sputtering flashes into an ambush.

*Buffalo Bill (1846-1917) — an early pony
express rider, served in the Union army
during the Civil War, created Buffalo
Bill's Wild West show
slanting — at an angle*

Early Moon

The baby moon, a canoe, a silver papoose canoe, sails and sails in the
Indian west.

A ring of silver foxes, a mist of silver foxes, sit and sit around the Indian
moon.

One yellow star for a runner, and rows of blue stars for more runners,
keep a line of watchers.

O foxes, baby moon, runners, you are the panel of memory, fire-white
writing tonight of the Red Man's dreams.

Who squats, legs crossed and arms folded, matching its look against
the moon-face, the star-faces, of the West?

Who are the Mississippi Valley ghosts, of copper foreheads, riding wiry
ponies in the night? — no bridles, love-arms on the pony necks, rid-
ding in the night a long old trail?

Why do they always come back when the silver foxes sit around the
early moon, a silver papoose, in the Indian west?

papoose — an infant or very young child in Native American culture
Indian moon — In Native American thought, each month was described as a type of
moon (e.g., Moose Hunter Moon, Corn Maker Moon, Freezing River Maker Moon).

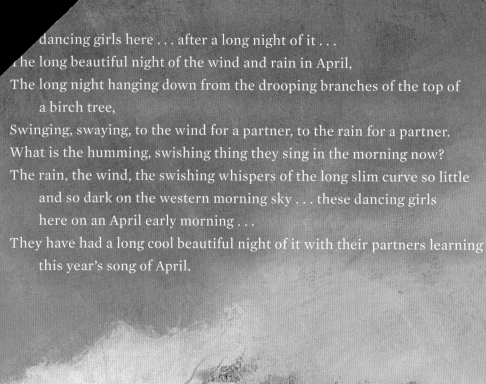

dancing girls here . . . after a long night of it . . .
The long beautiful night of the wind and rain in April,
The long night hanging down from the drooping branches of the top of
 a birch tree,
Swinging, swaying, to the wind for a partner, to the rain for a partner.
What is the humming, swishing thing they sing in the morning now?
The rain, the wind, the swishing whispers of the long slim curve so little
 and so dark on the western morning sky . . . these dancing girls
 here on an April early morning . . .
They have had a long cool beautiful night of it with their partners learning
 this year's song of April.

Washerwoman

The washerwoman is a member of the Salvation Army.
And over the tub of suds rubbing underwear clean
She sings that Jesus will wash her sins away
And the red wrongs she has done God and man
Shall be white as driven snow.
Rubbing underwear she sings of the Last Great Washday.

*Salvation Army — an international
charitable organization founded
by Methodists in 1865 in London.
They seek donations, especially at
Christmastime, when volunteers
ring their bells by red buckets.
Last Great Washday — a metaphor
for Final Judgment Day*

Psalm of Those Who Go Forth before Daylight

The policeman buys shoes slow and careful; the teamster buys gloves slow and careful; they take care of their feet and hands; they live on their feet and hands.

The milkman never argues; he works alone and no one speaks to him; the city is asleep when he is on his job; he puts a bottle on six hundred porches and calls it a day's work; he climbs two hundred wooden stairways; two horses are company for him; he never argues.

The rolling-mill men and the sheet-steel men are brothers of cinders; they empty cinders out of their shoes after the day's work; they ask their wives to fix burnt holes in the knees of their trousers; their necks and ears are covered with a smut; they scour their necks and ears; they are brothers of cinders.

Psalm — sacred song or poem of praise
rolling-mill men and sheet-steel men — they make metal
into flat pieces used in construction of cars and airplanes,
tin roofs. Smaller, thinner metal like gold and silver is used
to make jewelry.

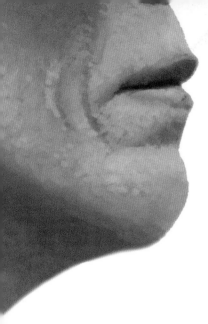

People with Proud Chins

I tell them where the wind comes from,
Where the music goes when the fiddle is in the box.

Kids — I saw one with a proud chin, a sleepyhead,
And the moonline creeping white on her pillow.
 I have seen their heads in the starlight
 And their proud chins marching in a mist of stars.

They are the only people I never lie to.
 I give them honest answers,
Answers shrewd as the circles of white on brown chestnuts.

shrewd — good at judging people and events; clever

Hits and Runs

I remember the Chillicothe ball players grappling the Rock Island ball
    players in a sixteen-inning game ended by darkness.
And the shoulders of the Chillicothe players were a red smoke against the
    sundown and the shoulders of the Rock Island players were a yellow
    smoke against the sundown.
And the umpire's voice was hoarse calling balls and strikes and outs and
    the umpire's throat fought in the dust for a song.

*Chillicothe and Rock Island — towns in Illinois where minor league baseball teams played
sixteen-inning games — usually ball games consist of nine innings; this game has been tied since the
ninth inning and the teams continue to play for a winner.*

Poems about Places

Fog

The fog comes
on little cat feet.

It sits looking
over harbor and city
on silent haunches
and then moves on.

haunches — the upper part of an animal's rear legs

Young Sea

The sea is never still.
It pounds on the shore
Restless as a young heart,
Hunting.

The sea speaks
And only the stormy hearts
Know what it says:
It is the face
     of a rough mother speaking.

The sea is young.
One storm cleans all the hoar
And loosens the age of it.
I hear it laughing, reckless.

They love the sea,
Men who ride on it
And know they will die
Under the salt of it.

Let only the young come,
     Says the sea.
Let them kiss my face
     And hear me.
I am the last word
     And I tell
Where storms and stars come from.

hoar — a weather phenomenon in which ice crystals or water vapor freezes over objects and vegetation

Who Am I?

My head knocks against the stars.
My feet are on the hilltops.
My finger-tips are in the valleys and shores of universal life.
Down in the sounding foam of primal things I reach my hands and play
    with pebbles of destiny.
I have been to hell and back many times.
I know all about heaven, for I have talked with God.
I dabble in the blood and guts of the terrible.
I know the passionate seizure of beauty
And the marvelous rebellion of man at all signs reading "Keep Off."

My name is Truth and I am the most elusive captive in the universe.

universal life — life everywhere in the world
sounding foam — the sound of waves on the beach
primal things — things at the beginning of life or the world
destiny — the future; fate
passionate seizure — strong emotional grasp
elusive captive — hard-to-find prisoner or hostage

The Road and the End

I shall foot it
Down the roadway in the dusk,
Where shapes of hunger wander
And the fugitives of pain go by.
I shall foot it
In the silence of the morning,
See the night slur into dawn,
Hear the slow great winds arise
Where tall trees flank the way
And shoulder toward the sky.

The broken boulders by the road
Shall not commemorate my ruin.
Regret shall be the gravel under foot.
I shall watch for
Slim birds swift of wing
That go where wind and ranks of thunder
Drive the wild processionals of rain.

The dust of the traveled road
Shall touch my hands and face.

fugitives — people who run away
slur — smear + blur = slur
flank — stand next to something
shoulder — nudge
commemorate — honor
regret — something you feel sorry for
ranks of thunder — like soldiers standing in formation
processionals — formal celebrations or parades

Sunset from Omaha Hotel Window

Into the blue river hills
The red sun runners go
And the long sand changes
And today is a goner
And today is not worth haggling over.

    Here in Omaha
    The gloaming is bitter
    As in Chicago
    Or Kenosha.

The long sand changes.
To-day is a goner.
Time knocks in another brass nail.
Another yellow plunger shoots the dark.

    Constellations
    Wheeling over Omaha
    As in Chicago
    Or Kenosha.

The long sand is gone
and all the talk is stars.
They circle in a dome over Nebraska.

runners — streamers
long sand — reference to the prehistoric
time when the prairies were under water
haggling — arguing
Omaha — city in Nebraska
Kenosha — city in Wisconsin
gloaming — twilight, dusk
goner — dead
brass nail — used in coffins because they don't rust
plunger — pointer or indicator
Constellations — groups of stars forming shapes,
like the Big Dipper
wheeling — turning, revolving

Limited

I am riding on a limited express, one of the crack trains of the nation.
Hurtling across the prairie into blue haze and dark air go fifteen all-steel
      coaches holding a thousand people.
(All the coaches shall be scrap and rust and all the men and women
      laughing in the diners and sleepers shall pass to ashes.)
I ask a man in the smoker where he is going and he answers: "Omaha."

limited express — a fast train with few stops
crack trains — excellent trains
hurtling — going fast, racing
haze — mist or fog
diners and sleepers — special cars on a train
for eating and sleeping

Laughing Corn

There was a high majestic fooling
Day before yesterday in the yellow corn.

And day after tomorrow in the yellow corn
There will be high majestic fooling.

The ears ripen in late summer
And come on with a conquering laughter,
Come on with a high and conquering laughter.

The long-tailed blackbirds are hoarse.
One of the smaller blackbirds chitters on a stalk
And a spot of red is on its shoulder
And I never heard its name in my life.

Some of the ears are bursting.
A white juice works inside.
Cornsilk creeps in the end and dangles in the wind.
Always — I never knew it any other way —
The wind and the corn talk things over together.
And the rain and the corn and the sun and the corn
Talk things over together.

Over the road is the farmhouse.
The siding is white and a green blind is slung loose.
It will not be fixed till the corn is husked.
The farmer and his wife talk things over together.

fooling — tricking, joking, playful
hoarse — having a rough, grating sound
chitters — chatters, chirps
cornsilk — fine tassels on the top of ears of corn
slung — open, broken
husked — removed the husk (outer green leaves of corn)

Muckers

Twenty men stand watching the muckers.
    Stabbing the sides of the ditch
    Where clay gleams yellow,
    Driving the blades of their shovels
    Deeper and deeper for the new gas mains,
    Wiping sweat off their faces
        With red bandanas.

The muckers work on . . . pausing . . . to pull
Their boots out of suckholes where they slosh.

    Of the twenty looking on
Ten murmur, "O, it's a hell of a job,"
Ten others, "Jesus, I wish I had the job."

muckers — workers who remove dirt and waste
gleams — shines brilliantly
new gas mains — 1900-1914 in Chicago, underground
pipe systems were built to provide energy
suckholes — When muckers worked in mud, their boots
made a sucking sound when they walked.

Picnic Boat

Sunday night and the park policemen tell each other it is dark as a
    stack of black cats on Lake Michigan.
A big picnic boat comes home to Chicago from the peach farms of
    Saugatuck.
Hundreds of electric bulbs break the night's darkness, a flock of red and
    yellow birds with wings at a standstill.
Running along the deck-railings are festoons and leaping in curves are
    loops of light from prow and stern to the tall smokestacks.
Over the hoarse crunch of waves at my pier comes a hoarse answer in
    the rhythmic oompa of the brasses playing a Polish folk-song for the
    home-comers.

*Lake Michigan — one of the Great Lakes;
Chicago is on the southwestern shore
Saugatuck — a city in Michigan on the east
shore of Lake Michigan; in the early 20th
century, it was the destination of weekend
vacationers from all the Midwest.
festoons — garland decorations
prow — front of boat
stern — back of boat
rhythmic — having a recurring pattern of
sound*

Harvest Sunset

Red gold of pools,
Sunset furrows six o'clock,
And the farmer done in the fields
And the cows in the barns with bulging udders.

Take the cows and the farmer,
Take the barns and the bulging udders.
Leave the red gold of pools
And sunset furrows six o'clock.
The farmer's wife is singing.
The farmer's boy is whistling.
I wash my hands in red gold of pools.

furrows — trenches in plowed fields

36

Haunts

There are places I go when I am strong.
One is a marsh pool where I used to go
          with a long-ear hound dog.
One is a wild crabapple tree; I was there
          a moonlight night with a girl.
The dog is gone; the girl is gone; I go to these
          places when there is no other place to go.

Theme in Yellow

I spot the hills
With yellow balls in autumn.
I light the prairie cornfields
Orange and tawny gold clusters
And I am called pumpkins.
On the last of October
When dusk is fallen

Children join hands
And circle round me
Singing ghost songs
And love to the harvest moon;
I am a jack-o'-lantern
With terrible teeth
And the children know
I am fooling.

Buffalo Dusk

The buffaloes are gone.
And those who saw the buffaloes are gone.
Those who saw the buffaloes by thousands and how they pawed the
  prairie sod into dust with their hoofs, their great heads down pawing
  on in a great pageant of dusk,
Those who saw the buffaloes are gone.
And the buffaloes are gone.

39

from "Smoke and Steel"

Smoke of the fields in spring is one,
Smoke of the leaves in autumn another.
Smoke of a steel-mill roof or a battleship funnel,
They all go up in a line with a smokestack,
Or they twist . . . in the slow twist . . . of the wind.

If the north wind comes they run to the south.
If the west wind comes they run to the east.
  By this sign
  all smokes
  know each other.
Smoke of the fields in spring and leaves in autumn,
Smoke of the finished steel, chilled and blue,
By the oath of work they swear: "I know you."

Hunted and hissed from the center
Deep down long ago when God made us over,
Deep down are the cinders we came from —
You and I and our heads of smoke.

funnel — smokestack on a ship

The Skyscraper Loves Night

One by one lights of a skyscraper fling their checkering cross work on the
     velvet gown of night.

I believe the skyscraper loves night as a woman and brings her playthings
     she asks for, brings her a velvet gown,
And loves the white of her shoulders hidden under the dark feel of it all.

The masonry of steel looks to the night for somebody it loves,
He is a little dizzy and almost dances . . . waiting . . . dark . . .

masonry — stonework

Valley Song

The sunset swept
To the valley's west, you remember.

The frost was on.
A star burnt blue.
We were warm, you remember,
And counted the rings on a moon.

The sunset swept
To the valley's west
And was gone in a big dark door of stars.

Between Two Hills

Between two hills
The old town stands.
The houses loom
And the roofs and trees
And the dusk and the dark,
The damp and the dew
  Are there.

The prayers are said
And the people rest
For sleep is there
And the touch of dreams
  Is over all.

The Year

I

A storm of white petals,
Buds throwing open baby fists
Into hands of broad flowers.

II

Red roses running upward,
Clambering to the clutches of life
Soaked in crimson.

III

Rabbles of tattered leaves
Holding golden flimsy hopes
Against the tramplings
into the pits and gullies.

IV

Hoarfrost and silence:
Only the muffling
Of winds dark and lonesome —
Great lullabies to the long sleepers.

rabbles — crowds, mobs
tramplings — crushing, flattening
hoarfrost — frost

River Roads

Let the crows go by hawking their caw and caw.
They have been swimming in midnights of coal mines somewhere.
Let 'em hawk their caw and caw.

Let the woodpecker drum and drum on a hickory stump.
He has been swimming in red and blue pools somewhere hundreds of
    years
And the blue has gone to his wings and the red has gone to his head.
Let his red head drum and drum.

Let the dark pools hold the birds in a looking-glass.
And if the pool wishes, let it shiver to the blur of many wings, old
    swimmers from old places.

Let the redwing streak a line of vermilion on the green wood lines.
And the mist along the river fix its purple in lines of a woman's shawl
    on lazy shoulders.

hawking — making a bird screeching sound; selling something
vermilion — bright orange-red color

45

Street Window

The pawn-shop man knows hunger,
And how far hunger has eaten the heart
Of one who comes with an old keepsake.
Here are wedding rings and baby bracelets,
Scarf pins and shoe buckles, jeweled garters,
Old-fashioned knives with inlaid handles,
Watches of old gold and silver,
Old coins worn with finger-marks.
They tell stories.

pawn-shop — a shop where the pawnbroker lends money and keeps personal property as guarantee
keepsake — souvenir; remembrance

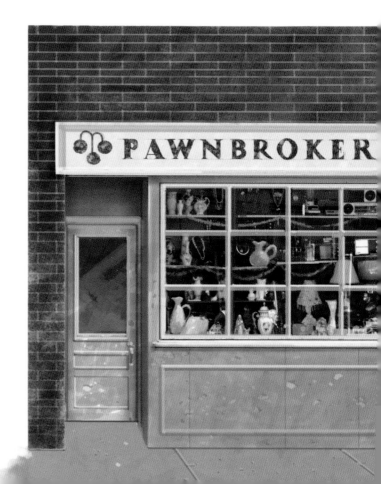

46

What Carl Was Thinking

Young Bullfrogs: Carl shows that a boy hears a bullfrog's sounds as music instead of just a croak. He demonstrates that Jimmy has an ear for music, and that it lingers in his head at the beginning of summer.

Weeds: Henry hoes his weeds because that is what the farmers in the area say must be done. Even though Henry knows the village's expectations, he still sees the strength in the weeds. And Henry knows that no amount of hoeing will ever really get rid of the weeds.

Soup: Depicting an ordinary event — eating soup — Carl shows us that all people are the same, even famous people.

I Am the People, the Mob: One of Carl's most famous poems. He rejoices in the strength and endurance of American people as they work together to maintain the American democracy.

Shenandoah: First, the Civil War battlefields from 1864 in the Shenandoah Valley are described as cemeteries where soldiers are buried. But then, after the passage of time, the fields are covered with wildflowers and grass, and speak of life.

Paula: This is Carl's love poem to his wife, Paula. He compares his poem to a song that celebrates his wife and especially her face. The song is sung from a pier to the depths of the sea.

Manual System: Imagine early telephone communication without cell phones or email. That early communication seemed like a kind of magic where people's voices materialized in odd contraptions.

Jazz Fantasia: The jazz music on a pleasure boat cruise on the Mississippi River is free-flowing and playful. Carl uses onomatopoeia as a poetic technique to create words that sound like an actual sound — "husha-husha-hush."

Illinois Farmer: The farmer wants to be buried on his own land, where he worked with his dreams.

Buffalo Bill: Buffalo Bill symbolizes the great American hero of the West. When he comes to town with his show, the parade is exciting for the young boys.

Early Moon: A baby moon, an early moon, is the beginning of the moon cycle. It looks like a small sliver or fingernail, "a canoe." This poem explores the potential of youth in terms of Native American culture.

Branches: The joy of spring is described by seeing and hearing branches move in the wind, like dancers.

Washerwoman: This washerwoman's work is like a gospel song calling for forgiveness.

Psalm of Those Who Go Forth before Daylight: We should praise those mill workers who keep our lives running smoothly through their sacrifices of backbreaking work, and little time for family and friends. They take pride in their work and never complain.

People with Proud Chins: Carl speaks about children's natural capacity to see the truth. Those children have strong chins and are not to be fooled with because they can see through lies and deceit.

Hits and Runs: Carl shows us how difficult it is for teams to play through an unusually long game, and for the umpires and fans too. When Carl was growing up in Galesburg, Illinois, he played baseball with his friends in a vacant lot.

Fog: Carl gives us a picture of fog as it creeps, stops, and moves on. It's a metaphor, comparing the fog to a slinking cat.

Young Sea: Carl imagines being young is like the movement of the sea, the salty ocean. Like the sea, a young person is restless, reckless, laughing.

Who Am I?: Carl looks for Truth in the heavens, on top of mountains, at the seashore. The natural world is a place to seek truth, knowledge of the universe.

The Road and the End: Life is like walking down a dusty path, during day or night. It is an adventure, a journey to experience the nature around us, and we get dirty with dust, with the touch of life.

Sunset from Omaha Hotel Window: Omaha, Nebraska, depicts a wide-open view of the Earth, the vast landscape of the Great Plains. Carl celebrates the wonder of this world, its past and present found where the sky meets Earth at the horizon.

Limited: In the early 20th century, limited trains were the fastest way to get from one place to another, generally stopping at larger cities, like from Chicago and Omaha. In the parentheses, Carl laments the loss of a culture when the trains are no longer useful.

Laughing Corn: "Majestic fooling" is a peculiar image that puts together unlikely ideas; a dignified joke. This poem compares the cornfield laughing playfully with the farmer and his wife.

Muckers: The muckers' work is portrayed as messy and dirty. But still people want those jobs in times of unemployment (1910s).

Picnic Boat: Carl describes the weekend pleasure boat that many Chicagoans took from Chicago across Lake Michigan to Saugatuck and Michigan's famous "Big Pavilion."

Harvest Sunset: "Red gold of pools" is mentioned three times to suggest a lovely, productive harvest.

Haunts: Carl describes the ways that places create our memories.

Theme in Yellow: Carl pretends to be a Halloween pumpkin to tell us how it might feel to be part of the Halloween celebration.

Buffalo Dusk: Carl laments the extinction of American buffaloes during the 1800s; it was a sad occasion in American history.

from "Smoke and Steel": All kinds of smoke mix together as the wind blows them. Our thoughts are like smoke that move around and mix together.

The Skyscraper Loves Night: The daytime image of the skyscraper's stone and steel falls in love with the nighttime image of the building as a graceful woman's figure wearing a sparkling evening gown.

Valley Song: As the sun sets in a valley, there is no horizon for the red, orange sunsets. We see just the slices of night in the stars above us.

Between Two Hills: People are protected by the hills that surround them and peacefully go to bed at night in a quiet village in a valley.

The Year: Each of the seasons is described from flowers and trees found at that time of year, how we see and hear those moments.

River Roads: On this road we find all kinds of birds that are full of color and sound. The birds are personified as people swimming in the nearby pool.

Street Window: All the items in a pawnshop have personal stories.

Index